The Knives We Need

The Knives We Need

Nava EtShalom

Carnegie Mellon University Press
Pittsburgh 2021

Acknowledgments

I'm grateful to the editors of these journals, where some poems in this collection were first published, sometimes under different names:

The American Poetry Review: "Recognition"
The Believer: "Charisma"
Blackbird: "Landing" and "Proposal"
Boston Review: "God of Suicides"
Court Green: "Conduct"
FIELD: "The Body Count"
The Journal: "Eclipse"
Vespertine Press: "Midwest Composition" (as "Composition")

Some of these poems also appear in the chapbook *Fortunately* (Button Poetry, 2020).

Book design by Martina Rethman

Library of Congress Control Number 2020951032
ISBN 978-0-88748-667-8

10 9 8 7 6 5 4 3 2 1

In memory of
Elias David Subar z"l,
poet

and

Amy Kaplan z"l,
teacher, fellow traveler, friend

You end up speaking all languages with an accent, even the distant one of your youth, the one you saved for love and anger.

—Breyten Breytenbach
"The Long March from Hearth to Heart"

Contents

III

Charisma

I'm more Mosaic every week: virtuously
burned, slow of speech. My brother
speaks for me. I am a brutalizer
of the brutalizer, a pillar of correctness
following a pillar of smoke and a pillar
of fire. I am slow of speech. I'll go
to the top of the mountain alone
for my epiphany, for my glimpse
of all the murderers and orchardists
to come, whom I have been defending
all these years under whatever laws
I can remember with my unbearable
face, that was young when we began.

I

God of Suicides

I have been wrong before, god of syntax
and understatement, god of slips in silk
and polyester, god of the laboratory, god of newsprint
and sunscreen, god of gulls, god of the unlocked bakery,
god of twins, god of all the cities of my youngest years,
god of the nurses who walk those wards, god
of sensible shoes and of Wall Street, god of whales
and their depths, god of the kitchen, god
of the blood clot, god of the authoritative sentence,
god of weight and liquor, god of scarves
and of the required fast, god of the green room
and the downbeat, god of lemons,
god of the disappeared and god of their mothers,
god of the highway's meridian, god
of all 206 bones and the compulsive catalogue,
god of freckles, god of rhinoplasty, god of narcotics, god
of the Five-Year Plan, god of the solemn
and the sudden, god of the stage,
god of runways, god of release on one's own
recognizance, god of the unrecognized face, god
of divorce and of lip gloss, god of crosswalks
and alphabets, god of M16s
and god of hands without instructions,
god of attention, god of the tucked
chin, god of the article,
god of the attitude, god of direction, god
of the brownstone and its master bedroom,
god of the pinstriped suit, the knuckles,
but in all of these furious declamatory years the question
has never been, god of what, god of the city's brick,
god of my palm, god of my open mouth.

Proposal

The promise of gravel, one skinned
arm and turned knee,
one bicycle and its wheels:

The chin-up of light,
morning gift in pine, this space
my palms describe:

The excellent refraction inside
whiskey, that unassailable place
we live within liquid:

The belly-up of fish all morning
on that morbid walk after
the tides have given up:

Those good citizens, the trees
and their branches, leaves that uncurl even
into our hostile spring:

The gazelle and its sister,
a gazelle; the other names for deer, ticked off
on our fingers:

The tent and the place we lived
inside it, two feet by two, and your hands
across my belly like lightning:

Landing

In Jerusalem a dead phone's dialed by exiles.
—Agha Shahid Ali

I

In a litany of safer places, we name hospitals,
highways, runways, where a body

is at least in motion. Sticking
hard to its own fable,

something simple about linen
and penmanship. The whole heart's

at work there, drawing dirt
from a garden of artichokes

for the eventual burial, far
from home, against a quiet sky.

2

The body and its constituent bones cross
dark oceans. These have names
and envelop the globe. Still,

they are standing in. Its smells
and inconstancies, its unwilled dissolutions,
leave our hands empty, leave our hands.

3

Our bodies go down
unwrapped, or all in white.

Conduct

I

I woke up from marrying my father;
the window let in a little streetlamp shine.

None of us knew what time it was.
The streetlamp thought three. The boy

thought morning, and started to wake.
I laughed. We returned to sleep slowly,

mouth to ear, and the marriages continued.

2

I was writing a poem when a boy blew up
and my fingers stopped on "matching boots."

Nobody has company now; what's one
lost body that was warm in my bed,

quilting a night of bad weddings?

3

I try to stay in sleep
where there is at least my body.

My temporary teeth, his neat hands,
an argument, a draft.

Waking I say I must
have imagined the weddings.

These pageants, these men, these buildings—
they go brightly on without me.

Materials

Gave a heart to fire, preferred
the hollow chest, filled

two hands with my body—
back-to-chest, palm-to-hip.

Two forgotten countries
carried on with local plans—

I never made anything
but a concession to thunder.

Anathalamion

I'm through with pronouncing my name,
arriving in doorways, skimming the room
for one quiet face, one dressed

body that casts no aura. Ten years ago
on a long white bed I was ready, I said
hello my name is, my arms were bare

for summer, you wore a cotton dress
you had sewn yourself, you were a mess
of August sweat and tied-off threads, I was scared

of innuendo but I lay down
when you told me to, on every side were chapels
and bells, but right there the town was silent,

ours. Enough, I should have said, tell me
my new name, but I have never—
you remember—saved anything for later.

Unfortunately

This side of the mountain's turning
toward night and the green blazes have faded,

I'm supposed to be the calm one, your hand
when I hold it warms me through, we have never been

enough company, you buried the keys
with dog zeal and I wish you'd like me less,

it's a series of left turns, when the house comes into view
it's the wrong one after all. All my bets have been bad bets.

Injury

I'm still asleep one afternoon in nineteen eighty-three
in a bed made of packing crates, eyes closed

against the serious light. This is the last improvised house
at the edge of town. We have two guns, no money,

and a waterbed. I know we have this quilt
and one fan against the heat. I don't know

who lives here with us. There's the new baby, and
there's the border. Everything we have, we guard.

Everything we have, we stole. I'll wake up
in a wash of sun—the desert fades to white.

Eclipse

This is a face that hasn't been used
for anything yet. It's so good to look at.
It hasn't seen the moon, hasn't leaned in
too far, hasn't pursed itself when the rain arrived
suddenly, hasn't ground its teeth
through a bad night, hasn't blushed or apologized
or brazened it out, has never sung, hasn't creased
in sleep, hasn't kissed any salt
or opened itself wide with surprise
at the things someone else's tongue can do.
This is the face that keeps repeating itself
across the screen like an apology
an apology an apology an apology. This is
the end, masquerading as the beginning.

II

Certainly

The call is bad news, both dogs are panting, the afternoon
is punctuated by sudden sleep, I hang a navy dress by the shower
which does nothing to shake its wrinkles out, and I mind

as if the dead mind. Or we have fish on Fridays—
in this version I seem to be Catholic—or
only my richest friend survives the wreck, or I count the funerals

I will and won't fan myself at, weep tidily through, cry
too loud at, be dead before, or that was the only love I had
after all, and all other loves paled next to it, or

the semblance of democracy gave out and we scrambled
for what food was left, in cans—what water,
caught in tarps, or I never saw 36, or 27, or adulthood

fizzled too quickly into age, and I kept putting off my suicide
to spare my mother's feelings, procrastinated
until I stood at her grave with dirt from Jerusalem in my fist,

redeemed from statehood, and we reminded each other
to throw, or we have cultivated imagination and hopelessness
in heaps and spades, and where have they gotten us.

Philtrum

God touched you there, and you forgot
everything you knew about the sea's dark floor
and its cities, about Pythagoras and his tight

hold on space, everything
about barbed wire on cattle-ranches
and at the border, about fish, how paint

sticks to plaster, the muscles
in a typesetter's arm, French, how to tie
a thief knot, the weather in the places

God took you, clouded and dense.
God pushed the skin above your lip—
was there honey on his finger? Did he

ask your mouth's permission?
Did you speak? Out of that long
river of forgetting, you were born.

Repair

All possible mistakes were made. Against advice,
the very pregnant boarded planes. Our monitors reported

the year as nineteen hundred. A delicate uncle tore his palm
on barbed wire, he was not freed. An aunt announced

her suicide plans, she was not accompanied. We mistook rigor
for a sign of health. At our feet

the sidewalk began to give in to the prairie, which looked like
a gesture of forgiveness. The sea unrolled in front of us,

its gifts of fish were accepted
and dressed and served. Ordinances were broken,

and dishes, fences, parameters, pledges. Again
we could never decide: when to say yes, what to rip,

what to build, what to destroy, when to reach for the knife, which
disobedience would save us.

Iteration

Knowing what I know, I still want

children. Two, with complementary

rages. Deep fjords

through the heart. This side

of the backseat, that side, the life

and the death of me:

one holy committee, one terror.

Yartzeit

I

Three notes on geography, left in our grandmother's
perfect Palmer method. Rochester.

Grand Rapids. Detroit.
Who placed spoons correctly,

her appropriate tongue. The myth of order
we've erected in her memory: stately cities

and the rivers they overlook.
Who could not sing, but did. Who believed

in justice as in her own kidneys:
delicate, bloody, laboring.

2

In the guest room, I check my body,
yours. The private use

of being born with an other.
Sibling inventories: fingers, shoulders, knees.

The last stop was her spine, something
akin to cancer, hunger. Nerve endings

sending the difficult instructions on.
Mapping us, finally, from the world to come.

Composition

I'm coming home on the Lake Shore line
with Rochester behind me, buckled at my neck
like my grandmother's evening cape.

The wide windows give up small
weather, a wet town, the next one
dry, no more news than that out here.

My grandmother with the stubborn
survivor's well-stocked pantry,
my grandfather whose sentences

never end, who shovels the driveway
with purpose over the sturdy years.
A small man costumed

in a city that stays still, the correct ear-flapped hat
for every morning's job. A small house,
never urgent. The quiet of his arms

saying goodbye; the never looking
at my wild face. I am only twenty-two
through Buffalo, Erie, Elyria—

I'm calling from the heartland, I say,
to the heartland, mine the only hand
on the blurred window: a tableau,
a tune, a signal of itself.

Departure

We push off from the narrow pier
in a narrow vessel, unhelmed. In the hold
we've brought compasses, packed sandwiches,

tarps, melamine, laminate,
aluminum—our mothers' materials—mildew,
what do we know,

collected. Quiet and low,
the sound of traffic beyond the trees
is a balm. We'll lay our parents down

on the bad Tuesday, so now we practice
an amphibian gesture, against belonging.
We'll go down too, remembered after

by our knuckles, our jaws, our plasticized maps,
our forbears, meticulously psalmed.

At the Jerusalem Hotel

We drink fizzy water, we're still too young,
you smoke Gauloises. Your mobile face

is a relief after the guarded stone entrances
where I have spent my afternoon.

I fill and empty our glasses,
you trace a pattern of old sugar

on the tabletop, you click your constant
tongue. I have been visiting tombs

where the bones of the patriarchs may
or may not be. I have been speculating

on ancient skeletons. Certainly
there was a soldier with rolled sleeves

and trained thighs. He posed
outside of time there

against the low wall with his M16,
he asked me about my name

and found me, as you do,
familiar. We were the same age

in front of Jacob's tomb.
He had my grandfather's eyes

(the old joke—he can't see)
and my father's gun (the old

joke—). He had everything my mother stole

and sold. Looking like me—

you look up—is the surest sign
of danger. Here, I've brought us postcards

from Bethlehem and mild soaps from Nablus,
smelling of olives and their afterlives. Around us,

marching ruthlessly over the hills, a column of pine
planted in our honor. Our best betrayals

are still before us. Later, elsewhere, otherwise:
our cousin thieves, the prohibition against grief.

Succession

His mouth was open. I thought
he would close it. A little privacy
before God and me at the last minute.

His hands were open, fingers long
as always. Head bare.
He looked me in the mouth

and wanted me to kiss him.
He stood too close, I stood too close.
When the angel saved him

I missed the red gush arriving.
I taught Judas in my later years how
to touch the mouths of the about-to-die.

Inheritance

In this version I live in Los Angeles,
I wear green and a moth halo, I keep
my lisp and I'm pregnant with my second,

my third, now monthly I visit
the baths where I like the lady best
and the freckles on my back seen by every

summer stranger are in this version seen
only by her. I love the Friday bustle,
setting flares for tomorrow,

setting some things to warm
and others to freeze but this week we'll go
to my mother's, who in this version

is married and heterosexual and covered
and cooking, and what does that make
my mother, who should have left

in nineteen eighty-five, how small
has she become, how strange, what disease
is claiming her, do we

serve the meal on paper, she fades
so early now, this week do I say goodbye
after dinner with the flick

of the eyes we know means be careful,
and when this version's husband leaves
on Saturday to kneel and sing without me,

does he have my father's red beard or the text
under his fingernails, when he comes home at noon
do I accede to his claims

which are radiant and serve lunch,
thinly sliced and salted,
in this version as in that does he

say sorry after or in this version as in that
will he never admit the thing he's done,
and done again, or will he look at me exasperated

in this version as in that, encompass all my rage
and love and nausea with his palm and say
why don't you just leave, if I'm as terrible

as you say. In this version as in that,
I believe I am articulate, and in every version,
I am just his iterating prayer.

After the Fire

after Paul Celan

I am black and lovely like
the tents of Kedar, like the curtains

of Solomon, lovely like the dark
tents of Solomon, lovely like the daughters

of Jerusalem. And if I forget thee
Jerusalem may my tongue cleave

to the roof of my mouth,
may my left hand forget its cunning,

may my right, may my tongue
cleave may the daughters

of Jerusalem may the burnt curtains
of Kedar the tents

of Solomon, the light long since
dimmed, the place we have long since

returned to, Solomon ashen,
Kedar, Shulamit

A heart like the heart of a fruit
A skin like the skin of a fruit

The Binding of Isaac

It was afterward
Abraham. Take

and make of him a hillside
I will show you.

Abraham saw
the place from afar. Said

return the wood for the offering,
Isaac; the fire and the knife,

both of them. My father—
my son. I see the fire;

and the wood? God will provide
both of them.

Abraham arranged the wood
on the wood. Abraham

stretched his knife
of God: Abraham,

Abraham.
Here I am, and we still.

Recognition

I'll cede ground that isn't mine.
I'll make my grandparents' apologies,
I'll make my own, since they're still here
taking constitutionals, surveying. Even
my renunciations are cribbed.
We think we own our graves

on the Mount of Olives, graves
in the hills beyond Jerusalem, doorbells
along the old streets where my name appears,
and at the corner somebody surprises me
wearing my face. Who's to say whose.
Here's capital and all its homelessness.

We've paid for our graves up front
with a view of the messiah. We're living
in the waiting room. I've changed
the allegiance of my plural pronoun, given up
my primordial lisp. A great theft made me, and now
this is no place for family life.

Holy Committee

We cut it down from the taut rope, you and I, we checked its pockets for a name, we prepared it for the clean white cloth. We took its thin clothes off, but that was not enough, nor was the careful bath, nor the laying-out on old tile, nor our hands over its eyes, our warm skin, my fingers notched between your teeth, your jaw fastened around my shoulder's bones. None of us were ready. The sun began anyway to set into the low kitchen window, the moon making a late arrival. The moon is not a person. The rock is not a moon, the years it took to release my arm from yours is not an allegory, it is the body dissolving, the way we look at once smoother and older in the evening, in our private mirrors. It was a dark afternoon, but something brightened in the city and the body, head unspeakable, toes in the soup, turned into view.

Delivery

That stupid interrupting ram when I had just reached both arms up to heaven and my legs were weak beneath me—

Rendition

My grandmother served dinner in pearls, and the guests wore pearls, and everyone with their dark tidy hair, everyone in their Peter Pan collars—if there were beets, they were from a can. Meanwhile her husband at the turkey, meanwhile the Dictaphone and butterscotches in the study, meanwhile the pile carpet in salmon, her son in the garage.

2

In our distant desert house, I was buttoning and unbuttoning. We had a homemade bunk bed there. A bright rug, a guard tower, an Uzi, an access of metaphor. Dahlias and sprinkler systems. I was learning snap closures, and the phone rang, and my mother picked it up.

3

In her pocketbook and pumps opened the garage, held the heavy bent handle and turned it, heaved the door up and her son lay on the floor where he was dead. Meanwhile the car's unapproachable fumes—then a pale announcement, a weak lie, everybody's ghost sits for dinner in everybody's chair.

The Body Count

1 Out of Which a Noise Came

Nothing on television answered
even one

in the series of questions: who was left
standing, and how

were they arranged? Who will reassemble
the limbs and fingers

we have on file, boxed
and waiting?

Better not—

2 *With Whom I Was in Love While I Was in Love with You*

Did I conduct the electricity or just
describe it? I remember

a series of bodies pitted against mine.
I don't remember who invited them,

or what the arc of consent was.
The echo of it, the yes in stereo, the magnets

behind our breastbones.
The keys in our palms.

The backs of whose knees hummed—I wanted
that shoulder in my mouth
the way I held yours; and it was small, and fit there.

3 *In Which We Believe*

The last day.
A series of last days:

horsemen.
Whose gesture is it?

The sky,
reliable for so long, ripped open.

Bronze

I had done nearly nothing. I had exhausted my visa. We went abroad, and I kept quiet. For one year I said the sound *r* over and over, in our way and in theirs, but nothing else. For two years I hopscotched, and snapped and unsnapped pink pajamas. For three years I learned spaghetti and toast. For four years I swept floors so the wood began to wear. We went home. We built a church to where we had been. We made a temple of its smells. We cooked its meat in its sauces, we invited its mothers for coffee, we kept our passports up to date. We're collecting events, but nothing ever happens here.

Archive

We're never right about the thing that matters
most, the thing we should scrabble through the nightstand for

when the house is burning—by each front door,
a suitcase; under each mattress, a lockbox; on each tongue

a very old word. Under one table-leg in four, the fold
of cardboard that keeps it straight. Better to have burned

with paper. Better to have burned like paper, quick delicate edge,
words briefly sharp against white, crumple

into an illegible orb. Better to have burned
for paper, to have given up this brief decipherable body.

Patronym

Someone approaches wearing my name and the old rage
returns. I've been making plans to trade mine in
for something less recognizable—something the understanders
will not understand. The sins, as they say, of the—
The air is thick with it, a pale violent pollen.
Better to be unpronounceable, I wonder, than to be seen.

Fortunately

We left in time, the door
locks by itself, the heat was low,

on Fridays the mail comes early,
each of us has a younger sister,

no photographs have been passed down
on my side, no obligations

on yours, no snow is predicted, you drank two
whiskey and sodas, you didn't

drink three—or stand there sober, expecting
something—and fire crept more slowly

than I thought it could from pole
to electric pole.

Arrival

On the ship's manifest, there are matches
and maps wrapped against the weather;
blankets, boots, hooks of all sizes—

for grappling, for fish, for fastening.
Pencils, soap, gunpowder,
envelopes and lengths of chain.

Powdered milk and cured olives, all
the knives we'll need. Skirts as thin
as nothing, subject to the wind. Everyone

arrives silent at the rails. Some hands, some
rescued palms to palms, some barely kept
from leaping over. As night

sets in, bread and salt, we watch the land,
the tall candles burning welcome. Those are only gulls
shaped like us, waiting on the rocks.

Of Ceos

There's the olive tree, and what was left beneath it.
It's October and time to lay down the canvas.
But damn the tables laid out in parallel, damn one guest
leaning close to another's ear with a question
that keeps unfolding mouth to mouth, damn
the last thing the last guest chewed and swallowed, damn
the ceiling and the pillars and the foundation, damn
Simonides, stepping outside, damn the banquet guests
who died, damn the messengers, damn the blood the ground
absorbed, damn Castor, damn Pollux in absentia, damn every map
drawn later. Damn lemon balm, the silver underside
of the olive, damn rosemary most of all, that's for—
The library burned at Alexandria. Among the ashes,
uncatalogued, praise god for the art of forgetting.

Before the Birds

I did—on the mountainside—tell him
we loved him, and God did, and tied

his hands behind his back, wide palms, tapered fingers,
with a local rope I had been keeping for just this occasion.

He liked the rope like I like a snug jacket, like he once liked
to sit in someone's lap. He liked the knife like we all like

finally to know we've been right: this is a disaster
and the end, thank God and the overcast morning, has come.

We'll do it how we do it. We'll stay with you
from death until the burial, the song, the empty trees.

Notes

Proposal
"Those good citizens, the trees" comes from *Trees As Good Citizens*, a book housed at the Prelinger Library in San Francisco that was a prop in a 2008 contest run by the Third Coast Festival.

Landing
This epigraph comes from a poem Agha Shahid Ali published as "Ghazal 1" and dedicated to Edward Said in the fall 1997 issue of *TriQuarterly*. It appeared later without the dedication and with an epigraph from Mahmoud Darwish, first as "Ghazal" in *Rooms Are Never Finished* and later as "By Exiles" in the posthumous collection *Call Me Ishmael Tonight*. The epigraph that appears in later editions is from Darwish's "The Earth Is Closing in on Us."

The Binding of Isaac
The biblical passage under erasure here is my translation of Bereishit/Genesis 22:1-14.

This book has been percolating for a decade. In the meantime I have become disabled, learned new things about interdependence, and cancelled a lot of plans. This won't be brief.

I'm grateful to the editors of these journals, where some of the poems in this collection were first published: *The American Poetry Review, The Believer, Blackbird, Boston Review, Court Green, FIELD, The Journal,* and *Vespertine Press.* Thanks to Button Poetry, which published the chapbook *Fortunately,* in which some of these poems also appeared.

Thanks to my poetry teachers: Martha Collins, especially and always, and the Oberlin College Creative Writing program's 2000-2004 lineup; the writers I worked with at the University of Michigan's MFA program, especially Khaled Mattawa, Keith Taylor, Eileen Pollack, and Michael Collier; and Carolyn Cohen at Masterman High School.

Thanks to Elizabeth Gramm, brilliant reader and beloved poet. And thanks to the readers I was so lucky to have when we were just beginning: Rachael Sarto, Megan Kruse, Lili Glauber, Erika Kulnys-Brain, and Sarah Green.

For their support, space to write, and gifts of beauty and time and money, thanks to the Pew Fellowships in the Arts, the University of Michigan, and the residencies at Willapa Bay AiR, Hedgebrook, and Ragdale.

Thanks also to the Unterberg Poetry Center at 92Y, and to Rosanna Warren for an introduction there that reminded me I was still a poet. Thanks to everyone at Carnegie Mellon University Press for bringing this book to life: Gerald Costanzo, Connie Amoroso, and Cynthia Lamb, and also to Heather Brown. Endless gratitude to Jessica Hurley, without whom there would be no book.

Deep thanks and love to all of these people:

My family of origin, my first words: Ima and Yonah. The family that grew: Barbary, Jesse, Elie, Steve, Zoe, Rosi, Raffi, Joey, Mozi, and Julie. The friends who are my family: Chana Joffe-Walt, Haley Michaels Pollack, Rosa W. Goldberg, Jenny Asarnow, Alissa Wise, Ariella Cohen, Noah T. Winer, Stefan Lynch, Irit Reinheimer, Hillary Blecker, Marj Friedman, Sarah Burgess, and Jessica Rosenberg. The kids: Lena, Micah S., Mars, Maya, Miles, Marion, Zora, Jacob, Micah R., Mona, Amira, Isaiah, Amos, and Leo.

Amy Kaplan, with credit for every good thing my brain can do and none of its excesses. Laura Finch, Jessica Hurley, Thomas Dichter, David Kazanjian, and Paul Saint-Amour, who connect me to the modes of thought I almost lost. My fellow travelers in crip time, including Caroline Henze-Gongola, Barbary Cook, and Jen Rock. My political homes over the years, the places where we've organized for a free Palestine, worked for restoration and reparation for settler-colonialism, and dreamed up visions beyond marriage and against militarism.

And finally, the constellation of people that keeps my body and soul together. Together they've paid my rent, answered offensive questions from the SSA, shared my despair, rage, and joy and let me share theirs, fought with the hospital billing department, and organized quiet unexpected house concerts.

This includes everyone listed above, in one way or another, and it also includes these beloved people: Claire McGuire, Matthew Lyons, Isa Goldfarb, Rebecca Vitali-DeCola, Sarah Zlotnick, Talia Young, Elinore Kaufman, María Alvarez, Adam Rothstein, Mica Root, MJ Kaufman, Sarah Kate Kramer, Marta Berg, Susan Saxe and Moon Smith, Helena Lipstadt, Dick Goldberg and Debbie Weinstein, Alexis Leiberman and Ilene Burak, Joel Loewenberg, Jesse Carr, and many Subars: Jud and Amy, Milayna and Jeff, Elcya and Avi, and my Bubbie, Chaya.

Here's to mutual aid beyond our private networks.